A **BIG** thank you to all my family and friends for their gentle persuasion.

This book is dedicated to **Mallory, Madison, Declan, Ella, Christian** and **Lochlan,** my **dear grandchildren** who opened up a whole new world for me – and to their loving parents **Erica, Todd, Tyler** and **Emily,** who always make me proud.

A special thanks to Erica McKeon who turned my photos into a book and to Matt Finnigan of Skyprint LLC (Kenosha, Wisconsin) who made my book into a masterpiece.

THE ADVENTURES OF TWINS MALLORY AND MADISON

"TUMMY TIME WITH GRANDMA"

Written by: Barbara Schuermann Stock Stuckey

This book is a production of Lizzie Blitz Company

www.lizzieblitz.com

It was a beautiful **SUNNY** morning

and our **GRANDMA,** who is also our Nanny,
was sitting in the big brown leather chair.

GRANDMA was watching us have **TUMMY TIME** like we do everyday.

Oh, by the way, my name is **MALLORY**......
I was practicing rolling over and **MADISON,** my twin sister,
was doing pilates on her tummy.

Yay! She did it, great job **MADDIE!**
(Sometimes I call her Maddie, she doesn't mind.)

I was just laying there resting –
so peaceful!

All of a sudden **MADISON** scooted over by me.

She seemed to be looking down at me and I was looking up at her.

What is happening here, my **GRANDMA** wondered?
She had never seen us make eye contact before.
We were just about to turn six months old.

Oh, I guess nothing---just by chance.
My **GRANDMA** continued to watch us closely
and this is what she observed......

MALLORY, do you mind if I take your hand and chew on it?

Sure **MADISON,** I don't mind. You're not hurting me.

That must feel
really good on
your gums since
we are both
teething.

Oh yes!
It feels soooo
good!

MADISON, I can't believe you are
still chewing on my fingers!

Please......just a
little longer
MALLORY?

Okay,
MADISON!

AWKWARD!

MADISON, is it okay if I take my hand out of your mouth now? It's been quite awhile!

Yes **MALLORY,** it's okay. Thank you, **MADDIE!**

MADISON, do you mind if I grab your dress to help me pull myself over? No **MALLORY,** I don't mind at all, thank you **MADISON!**

Oops!
I rolled back again.

Please **MADDIE,** let me try this one more time!
Okay **MALLORY.**

Nice try, but why don't you forget about it for today?
You can try again tomorrow.
Why don't we just play with these toys for now?

Okay **MADISON,** I like the blue ball, how about you? I like the blue ball too.

Oh no, the blue ball just rolled out of our reach!

Why don't we just play with the yellow ball?

Oops! There goes the yellow ball also.

Where is our
GRANDMA?

MALLORY,
let's play with the
red ring, it will not
roll away.

Yes, that looks
like a lot of fun
and it is also
very soft.

MALLORY, thank you for sharing with me, that is very nice of you.
You are very welcome, **MADISON!**

Why does **GRANDMA** keep taking our picture?

Oops, I need a little rest - this **TUMMY TIME** is wearing me out - that's okay **MALLORY,** you are doing just fine.

I am really having a lot of fun playing with you **MADISON.** I feel the same way about playing with you **MALLORY.**

It is so nice to have a sister who is so caring, supportive and willing to share. I think we are very lucky to have each other.

Now we are looking and smiling at each other for
the very first time. We can really see each other!
It was so dark inside Mommy's tummy.

I can tell we are going to have a great life together.
I love you already **MADISON!**
I love you too **MALLORY!**

I know we are going to be the best of friends and
have a lot of fun times growing up together,
with our family and friends.

MALLORY, I am so glad you are my sister.
Me too **MADISON!**

CPSIA information can be obtained at www.ICGtesting.com
Printed in the USA
BVIW12n0149180918
527799BV00005BA/13